Teacher

Huge Collection of Funny Jokes for Teachers

By Chester Croker

Jokes for Teachers

These jokes for teachers will make you giggle. Some of these jokes are old, some of them are new and we hope you enjoy our collection of the very best teacher jokes and puns around.

We hope you enjoy these funny teacher jokes. You will find many corny and cheesy teacher jokes to make you laugh.

If you're looking for funny teacher jokes you've certainly come to the right place.

We've got some great one-liners to start with, plenty of quick-fire questions and answers themed gags, some story led jokes and as a bonus some cheesy pick-up lines for teachers.

This mixture of teacher jokes will prove that teachers have a good sense of humor.

Published by Glowworm Press
7 Nuffield Way
Abingdon OX14 1RL

FOREWORD

When I was asked to write a foreword to this book I was flattered.

That is until I was told by the author, Chester Croker, that I was the last resort, and that everyone else he had approached had said they couldn't do it!

I have known Chester for a number of years and his ability to create funny jokes is remarkable. He is incredibly quick witted and an expert at crafting clever puns and amusing gags and I feel he is the ideal man to put together a joke book about our profession.

He once told me, "When you're a teacher you know that every day you will help someone improve their life."

He will be glad you have bought this book, as he has an expensive lifestyle to maintain.

Enjoy!

Ian Cooper

Table of Contents

Chapter 2: One Liner Teacher Jokes

I was caught studying the periodic table in English class. It was an elementary mistake.

I got called pretty yesterday and it felt good. Actually, the full sentence was "You're a pretty bad teacher." but I'm choosing to focus on the positive.

Teachers always tell us to follow our dreams, but they don't let us sleep in class.

Did you hear about the student who stole a calendar from the teacher's lounge? He got twelve months.

Math teachers have too many problems.

Kids who have one-to-one tuition are in a class of their own.

My teacher is cross-eyed. She can't control her pupils.

To steal from one person is plagiarism. To steal from many is research.

If a picture is worth a thousand words, then why shouldn't we judge a book by its cover?

My teacher told me I had failed my exam. I told him he had failed to educate me.

Yesterday, a teacher's wife asked him to pass her lipstick but he passed her a super-glue stick instead by mistake. She still isn't talking to him.

Teaching history is old news.

Decimals have a point.

A general rule of grammar is that double negatives are a no-no.

Did you hear about the cross-eyed teacher who got sacked because he couldn't see eye to eye with his students.

Time is a great teacher. Unfortunately it kills all its students.

An elderly teacher asked a student, "If I say, 'I am beautiful,' which tense is that?"

The student replied, "It is obviously past."

Teachers deserve a lot of credit. Of course, if they were paid more they wouldn't need it.

My teacher always tells me to follow my dreams, but she won't let me sleep in class.

A teacher friend of mine gave me some great advice, saying I should put something away for a rainy day. I've gone for an umbrella.

A teacher wanted to buy something nice for his boss, so he bought him a new chair. His boss won't let him plug it in though.

When I was in school, I cheated on my metaphysics exam. I looked into the soul of the boy sitting next to me.

My math teacher called me average. How mean.

My friend used to teach Computer Science but then he lost his drive.

Chapter 3: Question and Answer Teachers Jokes

Q: Why did the teacher write the lesson on the window?

A: *Because he wanted the lesson to be clear.*

Q: What's the longest piece of furniture in a school?

A: *The multiplication table.*

Q: Why did the students like their trigonometry teacher?

A: *He never gave homework and assignment.*

Q: Why did the student take a ruler to bed?

A: *Because he wanted to see how long he slept.*

Q: Why was the student's report card all wet?

A: *Because it was below C (sea) level.*

Q: What do you call a teacher without students?

A: *Happy.*

Q: What do you get when you cross a teacher with a vampire?

A: *Lots of blood tests.*

Q: What do you do if your teacher rolls her eyes at you?

A: *Pick them up and roll them back.*

Q: What kinds of tests do they give witches?

A: *Hex-aminations.*

Q: Why did the music teacher need a ladder?

A: *To reach the high notes.*

Q: What's a math teacher's favorite sum?

A: *Summer.*

Q: Why did the teacher wear sunglasses in class?

A: *Because the class was so bright.*

Q: Why are the Middle Ages sometimes called the Dark Ages?

A: *Because there were many knights.*

Q: What's do witches like best about school?

A: *Spell-ing.*

Q: Why was the cross-eyed teacher fired?

A: *Because he couldn't control his pupils.*

Q: How is a teacher like a judge?

A: *They both give out sentences.*

Q: What food do math teachers eat?

A: *Square meals.*

Q: Why did the student throw his watch out of the window?

A: *He wanted time to fly.*

Q: Who's the king of the classroom?

A: *The ruler.*

Q: Why didn't the skeleton go to the school dance?

A: *Because he had nobody to go with.*

Q: Why was school easier for cave people?

A: *Because there was no history to study.*

Q: Why did the boy study on an airplane?

A: *Because he wanted to get a higher education.*

Q: What's a teacher's favorite nation?

A: *Expla-nation.*

Q: What do you call a teacher who is happy every Monday?

A: *Retired.*

Q: Why did the teacher marry the janitor?

A: *Because he swept her off her feet.*

Q: What did the ghost teacher say to the class?

A: *Look at the board and I will go through it again.*

Q: Why did the cannibal teacher get disciplined by the principal?

A: *For buttering up his students.*

Q: Why was the geometry class always tired?

A: *Because they were all out of shape.*

Q: What is a teacher's favorite form of transport?

A: *A scholar-ship.*

Q: Why did the student take a ladder to school?

A: *Because he was going to high school.*

Q: Where do door-makers get their education?

A: *The school of hard knocks.*

Q: What do you call a music teacher with problems?

A: *Trebled.*

Q: Why did the teacher jump into a lake?

A: *To test the waters.*

Q: Why was the geometry teacher off school?

A: *Because she'd sprained her angle.*

Chapter 4: Short Teachers Jokes

The teacher asks, "Sonia, what part of the human body increases ten times when it is excited?"

Sonia blushes and says, "That's rude, I refuse to answer the question."

The teacher then asks Timmy the same question.

Timmy replies, "It's the pupil of the eye."

"Well done, Timmy," responds the teacher. "That's correct."

The teacher then says to Sonia, "First of all, you didn't do your homework. Secondly, you have a dirty mind. Finally, you're in for a big disappointment later in life."

One day a poor student surprised his teacher.

He said, "I don't want to scare you, but my Daddy says that if I don't get better grades soon, then somebody is going to get a spanking."

The teacher said to one of her troublesome students one day, "I wish you'd pay a little more attention."

The boy replied, "I'm paying as little as I can."

A science teacher calls up his local paper and asks, "How much does it cost to put an ad in the paper?"

"Four dollars an inch," a woman replies. "What is it you want to sell?"

"A three foot step ladder," said the teacher before slamming the phone down.

A father asks his son, "How do you like going to school my boy?"

His son replies, "The going bit is fine, and the coming home bit is fine too, but I'm not too keen on the time in-between."

My teacher pointed his ruler at me when I was talking in class today and told me there was an idiot at the end of it.

I asked him which end.

The biology teacher was busy lecturing his class about dissection.

He said to the class, "I will now show you this frog in my pocket."

He reached into his pocket and pulled out a chicken and avocado sandwich.

He said, "That's strange. I distinctly remember eating my lunch."

A teacher goes to the doctor with a hearing problem.

The doctor says, "Can you describe the symptoms to me?"

The teacher replies, "Yes. Homer is a fat yellow lazy man and his wife Marge is skinny with big blue hair."

When I was a toddler, my parents would always say, "Excuse my French" just after a swear word.

I'll never forget the first day at school when my teacher asked if any of us knew any French.

My teacher's a real wag.

She came in to class today and said, "We'll only have half a day of school this morning."

After we all cheered, she said, "We'll have the other half this afternoon."

Two boys were arguing in class one day when the teacher walked into the classroom.

The teacher asked, "What are you two arguing about?"

One of the boys replied, "We found a five dollar bill and decided to give it to whoever tells the biggest lie."

"You should be ashamed of yourselves," said the teacher. "When I was your age I didn't even know what a lie was."

The boys then gave the five dollars to the teacher.

A relief teacher stands up in front of the class and asks if anyone in the class is an idiot, and says that if there is one then they should stand up.

After a minute a boy stands up.

The teacher then asks him if he actually thinks he's an idiot.

The boy says, "No, but I didn't want to see you standing all by yourself."

The history teacher notices a student sleeping at the back of the class.

The teacher shouts to the sleeping student's neighbor, "Wake that student up."

The neighbor hollers back, "You put him to sleep; you wake him up."

My math teacher asked me why I was doing my sums on the floor.

I replied, "Because you told us to do them without using tables."

A mother asked her daughter, "What did you do in school today?"

The daughter replies, "We played a guessing game."

The mother says, "I thought you had a math exam today."

Her daughter says, "That's right."

My teacher asked me today, "If your Dad earned $1,000 a week and gave your Mum half, what would she have?"

I told him, "A heart attack."

When taking my maths exam I asked my teacher for some advice and he said that you should always read through the paper first.

That's the last time I will ever listen to him.

I was halfway through my horoscope when I heard the invigilator say, "Okay, exam over. Pencils down."

A teacher took his cross-eyed Labrador to the vet.

The vet picked the dog up to examine him and after a short while said, "Sorry, I'm going to have to put him down."

The teacher exclaimed, "Oh no. Is it really that bad?"

The vet replied, "No, he's just very heavy."

The parents were very disappointed in their son's grades.

The father lamented, "The only consolation I can find with these terrible grades is that I know he didn't cheat during the exams."

A girl comes home from her first day at school.

Her mother asks, "What did you learn today?"

The daughter replies, "Not enough. I have to go back tomorrow."

I went to school with cotton wool in both of my ears today, and my history teacher asked me why.

I replied, "You keep saying things go in one ear and out the other, so I'm trying to keep them in."

"I've just had a dreadful time," said a boy to his friends. "First of all I got angina, then psoriasis Just as I was recovering from that, I got appendicitis. They then gave me hypodermics, and then, arteriosclerosis followed by tonsillitis."

"Crikey. How did you manage to get through all that?" sympathized his friends.

"I really don't know," the boy replied. "It was the toughest spelling test I've ever had."

The answer to the exam question was "log(1+x)".

A student copied the answer from the student next to him, but he idn't want to make it obvious that he was cheating, so he changed the answer slightly, to "timber(1+x)".

A cleaner had just finished polishing a wooden corridor when one of the teachers asked if he could wlak on the floor as he needed to use the toilet.

The cleaner scowled at him, and said, "Just a minute, I'll put down some newspaper."

"That's all right, madam" he responded. "I'm house trained."

A student teacher was asked to fill out a questionnaire for the school.

One question said, "Give two reasons for entering the teaching profession."

The teacher wrote, "July and August."

The teacher explained to the class all about latitude, longitude, degrees and minutes.

The teacher then asked, "Suppose I asked you to meet me for lunch at 52 degrees, 3 minutes north latitude and 3 degrees, 12 minutes east longitude?"

After some silence, a student offered, "I guess you'd be eating alone."

In court, when asked for her occupation, a woman charged with a traffic violation said she was a school teacher.

The judge rose from the bench and said, "Madam, I've waited many years for a school teacher to appear before this court."

He smirked as he said, "Now, sit down at that table and write 100 times, 'I will not run a red light.'"

We had an exam in class today and afterwards the teacher said to me, "I hope I didn't see you looking at Ronnie's answers."

I said, "I hope so too."

A PE teacher is struggling to find a parking spot in the staff parking lot.

"Lord," he prayed. "This is driving me crazy. I'm late for class as it is. If you open a space up for me, I swear I'll go to church on Sunday."

Suddenly, the clouds part and the sun shines down onto an empty parking spot.

Without hesitation, the teacher says, "Never mind Lord, I've found one."

The father employed a private tutor to help his daughter's education.

After a year, he noticed a huge improvement in her marks at school.

"You have done a great job." he told the tutor. "Also, in order to thank-you for all you have done, here's 100 dollars to take the missus out to dinner."

Later that night, the doorbell rang and it was the teacher.

The man asked, "What's the matter, have you forgotten something?"

"Nope." replied the teacher, "I'm here to take your missus out to dinner like you asked."

A teacher was having trouble teaching arithmetic to one young boy.

He decided to use a real world example so he said, "If you reached into your right pocket and found a nickel, and you reached into your left pocket and found another one, what would you have?"

The youngster replied, "Somebody else's trousers."

A dog walks into a pub, and takes a seat at the bar.

He says to the barman, "I would like a pint of cold beer and a packet of crisps please."

The barman is amazed and says, "You should think about joining a circus."

The dog replies, "Why? Do they need teachers?"

The teacher asked a farmer's young son a match question.

She asked, "Suppose there were a dozen sheep and six of them jumped over a fence. How many would be left?"

"None," answered the farmer's son.

The teacher said, "None? You don't know your arithmetic."

The farmer's son replied, "You don't know your sheep. When one goes, they all go."

A 78 year old retired teacher was walking in the park one day when he came across a frog.

He leant down, picked up the frog, and began to put it into his jacket.

As he did so, the frog said, "Kiss me on the lips and I'll turn into a beautiful woman and show you a good time."

The elderly teacher carried on putting the frog in his pocket.

The frog croaked, "Didn't you hear what I just said?"

The teacher looked down at the frog and said, "Yes I did, but at my age I'd rather have a talking frog."

A teacher says to the class, "Whoever answers my next question correctly, can go home."

A boy immediately threw his bag out the window.

The teacher asks, "Who threw that?"

The boy says, "Me. I'm going home now."

The children were queuing for lunch in the cafeteria of a Catholic elementary school.

At the beginning of the line there was a large pile of apples.

A nun had written a sign, which she had placed on the apple tray.

The sign read, "Take only one. God is watching."

At the other end of the line was a large pile of chocolate chip cookies.

When the children got there, one whispered to another, "Take as many as you want. God is watching the apples."

I remember my teacher telling me that looking out of the window wouldn't get me anywhere.

Boy, did I have a smug look on my face a few years later when I handed him his burger and fries at the drive through.

A young child is in school, taking a true-false test and he is flipping a coin.

At the end of the test he is flipping the coin again.

The teacher comes over and asks, "What are you doing?"

The boy replies, "Just checking my answers."

Little Johnny returns from school and tells his father that he got an F in arithmetic.

His father asks, "How come?"

The son replies, "The teacher asked how much is 2x3?' and I said '6'"

His father said, "But that's correct."

The son said, "I know. She then asked me how much is 3x2?'"

His father asks, "What's the f*cking difference?"

The son replies, "That's exactly what I said."

A male teacher was talking to two of his friends about their daughters.

The first friend says, "I was cleaning my daughter's room the other day and I found a pack of cigarettes. I didn't even know she smoked."

The second friend says, "That's nothing. I was cleaning my daughter's room the other day and I found a half full bottle of wine. I didn't even know she drank."

The teacher says, "That's nothing. I was cleaning my daughter's room the other day and I found a condom. I didn't even know she had a penis."

A young girl came home from school and complained to her mother, "I was punished today for something that I didn't do."

The mother exclaimed, "That's awful. I am going to call the school about this. Tell me, what was it that you didn't do?"

Her daughter replied, "My homework."

A young female teacher is sitting at the bar after work one night, when a burly sweaty construction worker sits down next to her.

They start talking and the conversation eventually gets on to Armageddon.

The teacher asks the construction worker, "What would you do if you hear the sirens go off and you know you've only just got twenty minutes left to live?"

The construction worker replies, "Oh, that's an easy one – I am going to make it with anything that moves."

The construction worker then asks the teacher what she would do to which she replies, "I'm going to keep perfectly still."

A Sunday school teacher is concerned that his students may be confused about Jesus, so he asks his class, "Where is Jesus today?"

Graham raises his hand and says, "He is in Heaven."

Maria answers, "He is in my heart."

Paddy answers, "He is in our bathroom."

The teacher asks Paddy why he believes that.

Paddy replies, "Every morning, after my father gets up, he bangs on the bathroom door and shouts 'Jesus Christ, are you still in there?'"

Chapter 5: Longer Teacher Jokes

Rabbits

Teacher: If I give you two rabbits and two more rabbits and another two rabbits, how many rabbits have you got?

Paddy: Seven.

Teacher: Let's try this a different way. If I give you two apples and two apples and another two apples, how many apples have you got?

Paddy: Six.

Teacher: Good. Now if I give you two rabbits and two rabbits and another two rabbits, how many rabbits have you got?

Paddy: Seven.

Teacher: How on earth do you work out that three lots of two rabbits is seven?

Paddy: I've already got one rabbit at home.

Secrets

One day Mick was taught at school that everybody has secrets.

He thought he would see if he could take advantage of it.

When he got home from school, he said to his mother, "Mum, I know your secret. I know everything."

His mother was worried, and said, "Take this twenty dollar note, and say nothing about it to your father, okay?"

Mick replies, "OK" and leaves the room with a big smile on his face.

When his dad came from work, Mick says, "Dad, I know your secret. I know everything."

Numb, his father reached into his wallet and said, "Take this twenty dollar note, and say nothing about it to your mother, okay?"

Mick replies, "OK" and leaves the room with an even bigger smile on his face.

The next morning, on his way to school, he sees the postman and thought he would try his luck with him.

So Mick says, "Mr Postman, I know your secret. I know everything."

The postman then fell to his knees, opened his arms wide and said, "At last the secret is out. Come, come to me my son."

Religious Education

Brother and sister Jack and Diane are sitting in school one day.

Diane is asleep when the teacher asks her a question, "Diane, who created Heaven and Earth?"

Jack sees that Diane is sleeping and he quickly pokes her with a sharp pencil to wake her up.

"Jesus Christ almighty," shouts Diane.

"Correct," says the teacher.

Later in the class the teacher asks, "Diane, who created Adam and Eve?"

Diane is again asleep and Jack once again pokes her with his pencil to wake her up.

"Jesus Christ almighty," shouts Diane.

"Correct again," says the teacher.

Towards the end of the lesson Diane is asleep once more.

The teacher asks, "Diane, what did Eve say to Adam when she had so many children?"

Once again Jack pokes her with his pencil to wake her up.

Diane screams, "If you stick that thing in me one more time, I am going to snap it in half."

Worms Experiment

A Chemistry teacher wanted to teach his class a lesson about the evils of liquor, so he set up an experiment that involved two worms, a glass of water and a glass of whiskey.

The teacher said, "Observe what happens to these two worms."

He placed the first worm in the glass of water, and it moved about, twisting and seemingly unharmed.

He then placed the second worm in the glass of whiskey and it writhed in pain for a moment, then quickly sank to the bottom of the glass and died.

The teacher looked around the classroom and asked, "What lesson can we learn from this experiment?"

One of the pupils raised his hand and responded, "Drink whiskey and you won't get worms."

Caught Cheating

In class one day, the teacher called Simon Jones over to his desk after a test, and said, "Simon, I believe you have been cheating."

Simon was taken aback and asked the teacher to prove it.

The teacher said, "For the question 'Who was our first president?' the little girl that sits next to you, Sally, put 'George Washington,' and so did you."

Simon replied, "Everyone knows that he was the first president."

The teacher said, "For the question 'Who freed the slaves?' Mary put Abraham Lincoln and so did you."

Simon replied, "I saw something on TV about that the other day."

The teacher raised his eyebrows and said, "For the question 'Who was president during the Louisiana Purchase?' Mary put 'I don't know,' and you put, 'me neither'."

Three Friends

Ron is talking to two of his friends, Jim and Shamus.

Jim says, "I think that my wife is having an affair with a mathematics teacher. The other day I came home and I found a pocket calculator under our bed and it wasn't mine."

Shamus then confides, "Wow, me too! I think that my wife is having an affair with an electrician. The other day I found wire cutters under the bed and they weren't mine."

Ron thinks for a minute and then says, "You know - I think my wife is having an affair with a horse."

Both Jim and Shamus look at him in disbelief.

Ron sees them looking at him and says, "No, seriously. The other day I came home early and found a jockey under our bed."

Reunion

A group of 40 year old teachers discussed where they should meet for lunch. They agreed they would meet at a place called The Dog House because the barmaids had big breasts and wore short-skirts.

Ten years later, at age 50, the teachers once again discussed where they should meet for lunch.

It was agreed that they would meet at The Dog House because the food and service was good and there was an excellent beer selection.

Ten years later, at age 60, the friends again discussed where they should meet for lunch.

It was agreed that they would meet at The Dog House because there were plenty of parking spaces, they could dine in peace and quiet, and it was good value for money.

Ten years later, at age 70, the friends discussed where they should meet for lunch.

It was agreed that they would meet at The Dog House because the restaurant was wheelchair accessible and had a toilet for the disabled.

Ten years later, at age 80, the teachers, now all retired, discussed where they should meet for lunch.

Finally it was agreed that they would meet at The Dog House because they had never been there before.

Pulling Power

Carlo the property developer and his teacher buddy Danny, went bar-hopping most weekends together, and Carlo would often go home with a hot woman while Danny went home alone.

One week Danny asked Carlo his secret to picking up women.

Carlo replied, "When you're out on the dance floor and she leans in and asks you what you do for a living, don't tell her you're a teacher. Tell her you're a lawyer instead."

Later Danny is dancing with a woman when she asks him what he does for a living.

"I'm a lawyer," says Danny.

The woman smiles seductively and asks, "Want to go back to my place? It's just around the corner."

So they go to her place, have some fun and an hour or so later, Danny is back in the pub telling Carlo about his success.

"I've only been a lawyer for an hour," Danny snickered, "And I've already screwed someone!"

Train Passengers

A teacher, a lawyer, a beautiful lady, and an old woman were on a train, sitting two by two facing each other.

The train went into a tunnel and when the carriage went completely dark, a loud "smack" was heard.

When the train came out of the tunnel back into the light the lawyer had a red hand print on his face. He had clearly been slapped on the face.

The hottie thought, "That lawyer must have tried to grope me, got the old lady by mistake, and she slapped him."

The old lady thought, "That lawyer must have groped the young lady in the dark and she slapped him."

The lawyer thought, "That teacher must have groped the hottie, she thought it was me, and she slapped me."

The teacher just sat there thinking, "I can't wait for another tunnel so I can slap the lawyer again."

Chapter 5: Teacher Student Exchanges

Teacher: Which book has helped you the most in your life?

Student: My father's check book.

Teacher: I asked you to draw a cow and grass, but I only see a cow. Where is the grass?

Student: The cow ate the grass, sir.

Teacher: What are the four seasons?

Student: Salt, pepper, ginger and cinnamon.

Teacher: Why have you got cotton wool in your ears, do you have an infection?

Pupil: Well you keep saying that things go in one ear and out the other so I am trying to keep them it all in.

Teacher: You missed school yesterday, didn't you?

Student: Not a bit.

Teacher: Where's your text book?

Student: At home.

Teacher: What's it doing there?

Student: Having a better day than I am.

Teacher: What is the future tense of the statement: 'I had killed a thief'?'

Student: You will go to jail.

Pupil: Would you punish me for something I didn't do?

Teacher: Of course not.

Pupil: Good, because I didn't do my homework.

Teacher: Where was the Constitution signed?

Student: At the bottom of the page.

Teacher: What's the chemical formula for water?

Student: H I J K L M N O.

Teacher: What are you talking about?

Student: Didn't you say it was H to O?

Teacher: You can't sleep in my class.

Student: I know. But if you were a little quieter, I could.

Teacher: Why are you late?

Student: Because of a sign down the road.

Teacher: What does a sign have to do with your being late?

Student: The sign said, "School Ahead, Go Slow."

Teacher: Your essay on 'My Dog' is exactly the same as your brother's. Did you copy it?

Student: No, it's the same dog.

Pupil: I don't think I deserved zero on this test.

Teacher: I agree, but that's the lowest mark I could give you.

Pupil: Can I go to the bathroom?

Teacher: Only if you can say the alphabet.

Pupil: abcdefghijklmnoqrstuvwxyz.

Teacher: Where's the p?

Pupil: Half way down my leg.

Teacher: What is the longest sentence you can think of?

Pupil: Life imprisonment.

Teacher: Give me a sentence starting with I.

Pupil: I is........

Teacher: No. You should always say I am, not I is.

Pupil: OK. I am the ninth letter of the alphabet.

Teacher: I wish you'd pay a little more attention.

Pupil: I'm paying as little as I can.

Teacher: Why are you doing your multiplication on the floor?

Student: You said we had to do it without tables.

Teacher: I hope I didn't see you looking at John's exam paper.

Student: I hope you didn't, either.

Teacher: What is the outside of a tree called?

Pupil: I don't know.

Teacher: Bark, boy, bark.

Pupil: Bow, wow, wow!

Teacher: Take a seat.

Student: Where do you want me to take it to?

Teacher: Why were you late?

Student: Sorry, teacher, I overslept.

Teacher: You mean you need to sleep at home too.

Teacher: Why are you late?

Student: My parents were fighting.

Teacher: What does that have to do with you being late for school?

Student: One of my shoes was in my mom's hand and the other one was in my dad's hand.

Chapter 6: You Might Be A Schoolteacher If

you refer to adults as "boys and girls."

you believe "extremely annoying" should have its own box on the report card.

you know a hundred good reasons for being late.

you have no time for a life outside work from September to June.

you want to slap the next person who says, "It must be nice to work from just 8 to 3."

you encourage your spouse by telling them they are a "good helper."

you've ever had your profession slammed by someone who would never dream of doing your job.

you don't want children of your own because there isn't a name you can hear that wouldn't elevate your blood pressure.

when you meet a child's parents you ask yourself, "Why is their kid like this?"

when out in public you feel the urge to talk to strange children and correct their behavior.

Chapter 7: Questions You Don't Want To Be Asked

Why are cigarettes sold in gas stations when smoking is prohibited there?

Why do you need a driver's license to buy liquor when you can't drink and drive?

Why is lemon juice mostly artificial ingredients but dishwashing liquid contains real lemons?

If nothing ever sticks to Teflon, how do they make Teflon stick to the pan?

If you tied buttered toast to the back of a cat and dropped it from a height, what would happen?

If you're in a vehicle going the speed of light, what happens when you turn on the headlights?

Why doesn't glue stick to the inside of its bottle?

Have you ever imagined a world with no hypothetical situations?

How does the guy who drives the snowplow get to work in the mornings?

You know that little indestructible black box that is used on planes? Why can't they make the whole plane out of the same material?

What do you plant to grow a seedless watermelon?

When sign makers go on strike, is anything written on their signs?

Chapter 8: Differing Grades

Different departments grade exams in different ways:

History Department:
> Students get the same grade they got last year.

Religious Department:
> The grade is determined by God.

Statistics Department:
> All grades are plotted along a normal bell curve.

Philosophy Department:
> What is a grade?

Psychology Department:
> Students are asked to blot ink in their exam books, close them and turn them in. The professor opens the books and assigns the first grade that comes to mind.

Law Department:
> Students are asked to defend their position of why they should receive an A.

Computer Science Department:
> A random number generator will determine the grade.

Music Department:
> Each student must figure out his grade by listening to the instructor play the corresponding note (+ and - would be sharp and flat respectively).

Physical Education Department:
> Everybody gets an A.

Chapter 9: Teachers Pick-Up Lines

You're like a teacher and I am like a math book - you solve all my problems.

I didn't know angels were allowed in public schools.

If you were my homework I'd slam you down on my desk and do you.

Are you a math teacher? Because you've got me harder than calculus.

Hey, baby, your physical structures are out of this world.

If I had to write a report card on you, I'd give you straight F's....for Fabulous.

Chapter 10: Summary

Hey, that's pretty well it for this book. I hope you've enjoyed it.

I've written a few other joke books for other professions, and here are some from my electrician's joke book:-

Here are just a few sample jokes; these are from my electricians joke book:-

Q: What kind of van does an electrician drive?
A: A *Volts-wagon.*

Q: What do you call a Russian electrician?
A: *Switchitonanov.*

Q: What is the definition of a shock absorber?
A: *A careless electrician.*

About the Author

Chester Croker, known to his friends as Chester the Jester or Croker the Joker, has written many joke books, and has been named Comedy Writer of the Year three times by the International Jokers Guild. He hated school and was once caned for wearing red socks to school.

I hope you enjoyed this collection of teaching jokes. As you know, some were cheesy, but I hope they brought a smile to your face, and you found them funny.

support@glowwormpress.com is the email address if you have any gags that you'd like me to include in the next version of this book.

If you did enjoy the book, kindly leave a review on Amazon so that other teachers can have a good laugh too.

Thanks in advance.

Printed in Great Britain
by Amazon

42847904R00037